STOP! SNAKE

CAMILLA DE LA BÉDOYÈRE

Quarto Library

Quarto is the authority on a wide range of topics.
Quarto educates, entertains and enriches the lives of our readers—enthusiasts and lovers of hands-on living.
www.quartoknows.com

Author: Camilla De La Bédoyère
Editor: Ellie Brough
Designers: David Ball and Mike Henson

This library edition published in 2021 by Quarto Library.,
an imprint of The Quarto Group.
6 orchard Road
Suite 100
Lake Forest, CA 92630
T: +1 949 380 7510
F: +1 949 380 7575
www.QuartoKnows.com

Distributed in the United States and Canada by
Lerner Publishing Services
241 First Avenue North
Minneapolis, MN 55401 U.S.A
www.lernerbooks.com

A CIP record for this book is available from the Library of Congress.

ISBN 978 0 7112 6463 2

Manufactured in Guangdong, China TT052021

9 8 7 6 5 4 3 2 1

Words in **bold** are explained in the glossary on page 32.

CONTENTS

WORLD OF POISON

Nature is amazing, but it can also be nasty! Some animals may look cute and cuddly, but even they may have a scary surprise in store for anyone who gets too close. From tiny terrors to mighty monsters, these scary creatures have a secret weapon—and it's deadly.

This deadly secret weapon is called poison, and billions of animals have it. They use it to hurt or kill other animals that they want to eat, or who want to eat them. There are many different types of poison but the result is often the same for a victim—a slow and painful DEATH!

POISON FACTS

★ Squishy sea cucumbers stay safe by releasing a **toxic** butt bomb! Its insides shoot out of its butt and they spray poison.

★ Many plants contain poisons to stop animals from eating them. Berries from a doll's eye plant stop your heart from working if you eat them.

★ Australia has more venomous snakes than any other country. In most countries you are more likely to die from a bee sting than a snake's bite.

Poisons, or toxins, are substances that can make an animal unwell, and some poisons are much more powerful than others. Some animals are poisonous to eat, but others inject poison using teeth, claws, or spines. **Venom** is poison that is injected.

Did you know?

Pitohuis are the only poisonous birds. If a predator tries to eat a pitohui, its tongue gets numb and tingly!

Read the clues and examine the pictures. Can you keep a cool head and identify the deadliest animals? Decide when you should sit and watch, back away slowly, or run for your life!

Did you know?

A honeybee stinger can keep pumping venom for 10 painful minutes!

BEASTLY BUGS

These creepy-crawlies all look scary, but can you really judge a bug by its looks? Which one do you think is the most dangerous?

- Sit and watch
- Back away slowly
- RUN FOR YOUR LIFE!

BRAZILIAN HUNTSMAN SPIDER FACT BOX

SPECIES NAME: *Phoneutria fera*
LENGTH: Up to 5 inches legspan
FOUND: South America

Wandering spiders, like the Brazilian huntsman, are large, hairy, and very scary! Unlike spiders that build webs, they go out and hunt **prey**. If they are scared they raise their front two pairs of legs so their venomous **fangs** are in fullview!

BULLET ANT FACT BOX

SPECIES NAME: *Paraponera clavata*
LENGTH: Up to an inch long
FOUND: South America

Most ants can sting or bite, but just how dangerous can a little ant be? Remember that ants live in large colonies, so maybe this mini-beast has lots of friends to help it defend its nest from attack.

DEATHSTALKER SCORPION FACT BOX

SPECIES NAME: *Leiurus quinquestriatus*
LENGTH: Up to 3 inches long
FOUND: North Africa, Middle East

Scorpions are members of the spider family, but unlike their cousins they keep their venom at the end of their long, curling tails. They deliver it with a fast stab from that sharp, hooked stinger.

Bullet ants build their nests at the foot of trees in rainforests.

Sit and watch

Bullet ant

Bullet ants deliver one of the most painful stings in the world, but one bullet ant's sting won't kill you, and they are not particularly aggressive **insects**. The deadliest ants include bulldog ants. They cling to their prey with giant jaws and keep stinging with deadly venom.

Back away slowly

Death stalker scorpion

This yellow terror is not the biggest scorpion, but it is the deadliest. Luckily each sting contains just a small amount of poison, so it's rarely fatal. These scorpions also live in hot, dry deserts where there are few people.

Deathstalkers prefer to lurk under stones and in cool, dark places. If you don't disturb them, they will leave you alone.

This spider's bite is incredibly painful, and its venom can stop a person from breathing. Thankfully there is an **antivenin** available!

RUN FOR YOUR LIFE!

Brazilian huntsman spider

The Brazilian huntsman is a type of wandering spider, and many **arachnologists** reckon that this is the deadliest spider of all. It is an aggressive, fearless **invertebrate** that will bite anyone, or anything, that gets in its way. If you see this spider, it's time to scedaddle!

MARINE MONSTERS

Deadly beasts lurk beneath the ocean's blue waters. Can you figure out which ones are the most dangerous?

Sit and watch

Back away slowly

RUN FOR YOUR LIFE!

BLUE-RINGED OCTOPUS FACT BOX

SPECIES NAME: *Hapalochlaena lunulata*
LENGTH: Up to 8 inches from tip to tip
FOUND: Shallow waters of the Pacific and Indian Oceans

Meet a small but scary **mollusk** with a bad temper. When this octopus is angry it glows with bright blue circles on its skin. But does this dazzling display mean danger, or is it just a clever way to confuse attackers?

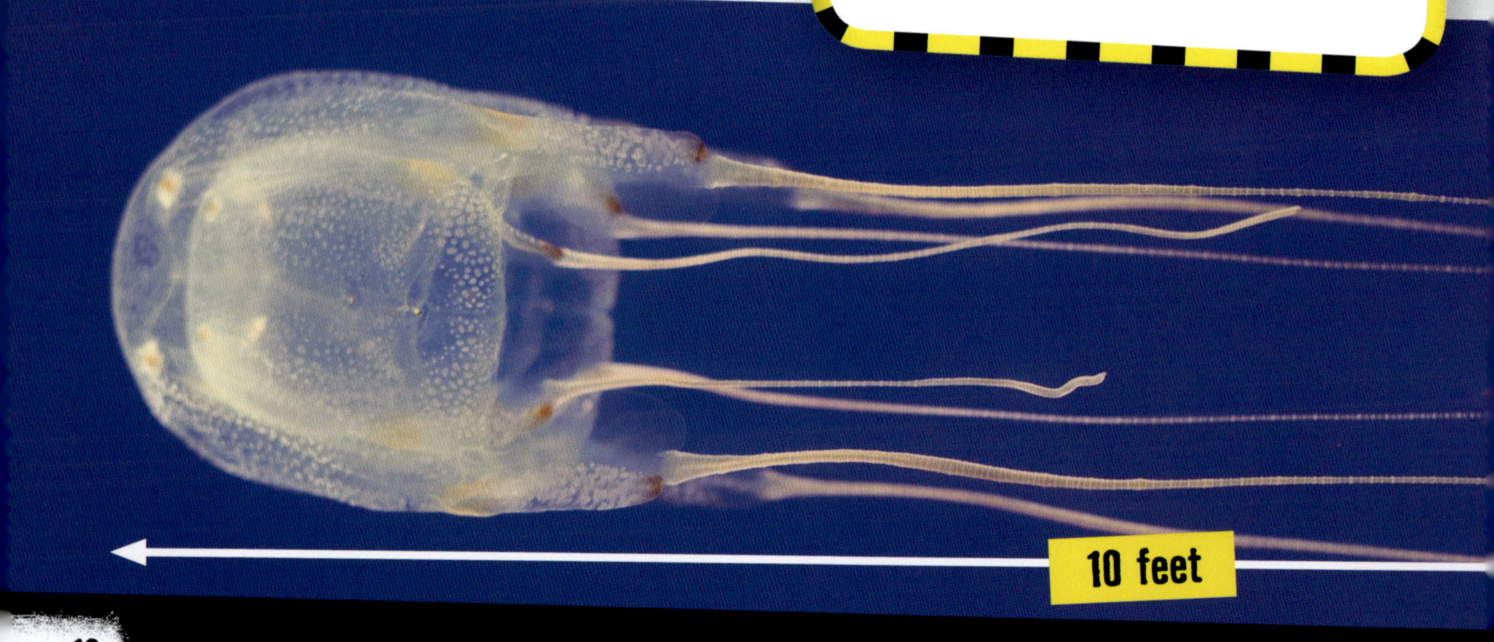

CONE SHELL FACT BOX

SPECIES NAME: *Conus spp*
LENGTH: Up to 8 inches long
FOUND: Warm coastal waters, worldwide

You could fit most cone shells into the palm of your hand, but holding one of these **marine** monsters is a bad idea. Cone shells are equipped with secret weapons, but are they killers?

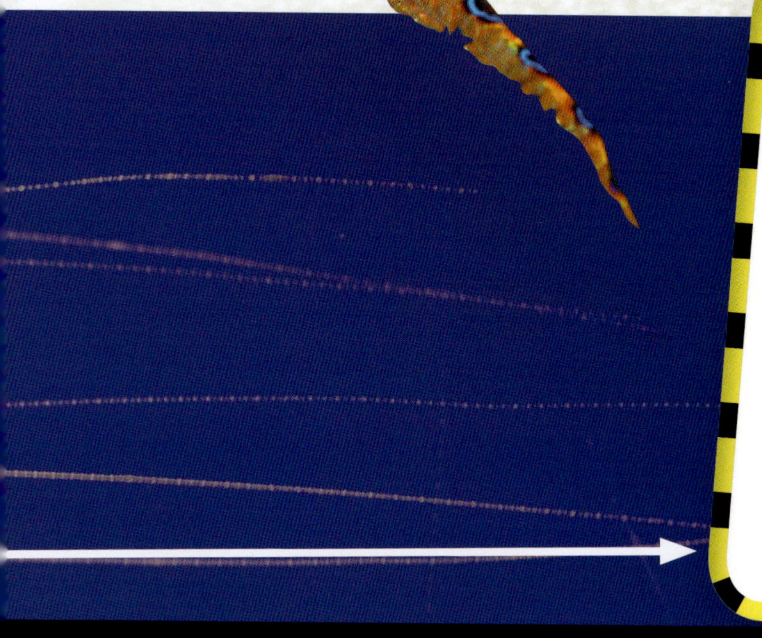

BOX JELLYFISH FACT BOX

SPECIES NAME: *Chironex fleckeri*
LENGTH: Up to 10 feet long
FOUND: Oceans and seas around Australia and Southeast Asia

This jellyfish is soft, slow, and squishy, with up to 60 long, trailing **tentacles** that dangle below a bell-shaped body. Just how threatening can a brainless, boneless jellyfish be?

Cone shells may be dangerous, but it's easy to avoid them!

Sit and watch

Cone shell

Few people would guess that a seashell could be a killer—but cone shells use a harpoon-like tooth to deliver a dose of poison. Their normal prey is fish, but if you handle one of these mini-beasts you could be targeted with one of nature's deadliest toxins.

Back away slowly

Blue-ringed octopus

This octopus bites so gently you may not even feel it at first—but its **saliva** is home to millions of bacteria that make a poison called tetrodotoxin (TTX). It only takes a tiny amount of TTX to kill a human.

The blue-ringed octopus is shy and hunts fish at night. It only bites humans to defend itself.

Box jellyfish hunt other marine animals, but humans can also swim into their tentacles by mistake.

RUN FOR YOUR LIFE!

Box jellyfish

Beware this beast! It is almost impossible to see it as it swims, and its tentacles are equipped with millions of microscopic stingers—each one loaded with venom. Once a victim is trapped in its tentacles the jellyfish fires off as many stingers as it can—with deadly effect.

FIERCE FISH

Should you fear colorful fish that like to be the center of attention, or **camouflaged** fish that prefer to stay hidden from view? You decide!

- Sit and watch
- Back away slowly
- RUN FOR YOUR LIFE!

LIONFISH FACT BOX

SPECIES NAME: *Pterois volitans*
LENGTH: Up to 12 inches long
FOUND: Warm oceans and seas

This impressive fish has zebra-like stripes, bright colors, and big, showy **fins**. Is it using color, shape, and pattern to just look beautiful to other lionfish, or is it telling everyone to keep a safe distance?

REEF STONEFISH FACT BOX

SPECIES NAME: *Synanceia horrida*
LENGTH: Up to 15 inches
FOUND: Indian and Pacific Oceans

This fish is beautifully camouflaged. It is doing a great impression of rocks and pebbles covered in seaweed! Stonefish live on the seabed around coral reefs where they hunt fish and small shrimp. Could this be a toxic killer?

STINGRAY FACT BOX

SPECIES NAME: *Taeniura lymma*
LENGTH: Up to 6 feet long
FOUND: Indian and Pacific Oceans

Stingrays are members of the shark family, and they are predators. Their **lethal** weapon is a huge stinger at the base of the tail. The stinger has a sharp spine that is lined with **barbs** and there is a giant venom gland at its base. Is this a gentle giant or a frightening fish?

Sit and watch

Stingray

This stingray may have all the equipment it needs to deliver a powerful dose of poison, but it's a shy and gentle fish that is only likely to attack to defend itself. Its poison causes great pain and damages muscles, but it is rarely fatal.

A stingray's sharp stinger is big—up to 8 inches long—but this fish prefers to swim away from danger.

Back away slowly

Lionfish

If this fish swims toward you, flashing its big fins, it's time to move away. It has 18 venomous spines which the fish uses to deliver venom that is very painful. This fish isn't shy and it will approach divers and swimmers. Always keep your distance from a lionfish!

There are 13 spines on a lionfish's dorsal fin, three spines in the fin below its tail, and one spine on each side.

RUN FOR YOUR LIFE!

Reef stonefish

A stonefish has the largest venom gland of any fish, and 13 spines to inject its dangerous poison. This fish's superb camouflage as it rests on the seabed adds to the danger because it is easy to tread on. The venom can kill in minutes.

A stonefish's spines are as sharp as needles and they can pierce shoes.

AWESOME AMPHIBIANS

This frog, toad, and newt have no spines, armor, claws, or teeth to defend themselves. They do have toxic skin though! Which **amphibian** do you think you should avoid?

Sit and watch

Back away slowly

RUN FOR YOUR LIFE!

CANE TOAD FACT BOX

SPECIES NAME: *Rhinella marina*
LENGTH: 6 inches long
FOUND: widespread in warm countries

This big, ugly toad was once found in Central and South America but it now lives in many countries where it is considered a pest. Is its toxic skin the secret of its success?

CALIFORNIA NEWT FACT BOX

SPECIES NAME: *Taricha torosa*
LENGTH: up to 8 inches long
FOUND: North America

A single drop of California newt's poison is enough to kill thousands of mice! Do you think this makes it the world's deadliest amphibian?

GOLDEN POISON ARROW FROG FACT BOX

SPECIES NAME: *Phyllobates terribilis*
LENGTH: Up to 2 inches
FOUND: South America

This beautiful little frog might make a nice snack for a passing lizard or snake, so why do predators steer clear of this amphibian?

This newt's jewel-like color warns predators not to eat it.

Sit and watch

California newt

The blood, skin, and muscles of this newt all contain a deadly poison, but the good news is that unless you feel like eating it, or at least licking its skin, you won't come to any harm in its company, if you can find one. These newts are shy and very rare.

Back away slowly

Cane toad

Cane toads were introduced to many countries so they could eat beetles that attacked sugarcane crops. They proved to be much worse pests themselves, as they produce milky venom that can kill all sorts of animals, from lizards to dogs.

When a cane toad is threatened it produces venom from glands behind its eyes and on its back.

RUN FOR YOUR LIFE!

Golden poison arrow frog

This frog lives in the rainforest, where it likes to sit on a tree root on a pile of leaves and trill loudly. It looks harmless, but its skin makes one of the deadliest poisons in the world. Rainforest people wipe their spears and arrows over these frogs' backs to make their weapons venomous!

The poison from this frog's skin can kill large animals—including people—in seconds.

RUTHLESS REPTILES

A toxic snake or lizard delivers its deadly dose of venom with its teeth, so it's best to steer clear of the head-end! Are you fast enough to outrun any of these scaly predators?

- Sit and watch
- Back away slowly
- RUN FOR YOUR LIFE!

MEXICAN BEADED LIZARD FACT BOX

SPECIES NAME: *Heloderma horridum*
LENGTH: Up to 3 feet long
FOUND: North and Central America

This venomous lizard climbs trees where it finds eggs to eat. It is a slow-moving lizard unless it sees something tasty or scary, but does it choose to attack or escape?

BLACK MAMBA FACT BOX

SPECIES NAME: *Dendroaspis polylepis*
LENGTH: Up to 11 feet long
FOUND: Africa

Black mambas are active in the daytime, hunting birds and small **mammals** on the ground. They strike with speed, but just how deadly are they?

FIERCE SNAKE FACT BOX

SPECIES NAME: *Oxyuranus microlepidotus*
LENGTH: Up to 6 feet long
FOUND: Australia

This snake is also known as the inland taipan and it usually hunts rats which it attacks by stabbing with its long fangs. Do you think this is a **reptile** that deserves its scary name?

Sit and watch

Mexican beaded lizard

When this lizard attacks it lunges forward at great speed, using its teeth to stab its prey and inject venom. Its venom is deadly to many animals but rarely fatal to humans. If you see this rare lizard you can watch it, but don't touch!

Venomous lizards have sharp teeth and their venom glands are in their lower jaws.

Back away slowly

Fierce snake

Fierce snake bites are extremely rare, and so far no one has died from one.

A fierce snake is the most venomous land snake in the world and it has enough venom to kill a hundred adult humans. So this is certainly a snake to stay away from! Thankfully it lives away from people and it is very shy, so you have time to escape.

RUN FOR YOUR LIFE!

Black mamba

The black mamba may not be as venomous as a fierce snake, but it has speed on its side. A mamba can move faster than you can, so you may not be able to outrun it! That makes it one of the world's most dangerous predators.

A mamba hisses and raises its head to warn if it is about to strike.

MAMMAL MENACE

Most mammals use teeth and claws to protect themselves, or kill their prey. These venomous mammal menaces are unusual, but are they deadly? You decide!

Sit and watch

Back away slowly

RUN FOR YOUR LIFE!

DUCK-BILLED PLATYPUS FACT BOX

SPECIES NAME: *Ornithorhynchus anatinus*
LENGTH: Up to 24 inches
FOUND: Rivers, streams, and lagoons of Eastern Australia and Tasmania

Looking like a cross between a duck and a beaver this mysterious animal belongs to an unusual group of egg-laying mammals, called monotremes. Male platypuses are deadly, but females are not—why?

VAMPIRE BAT FACT BOX

SPECIES NAME: *Desmodus rotundus*
LENGTH: Up to 4 inches long
FOUND: The Americas

Vampire bats are famous for sucking blood from their prey, but did you know that they need a meal every two days or they will die of starvation? They use toxic saliva to feed, but does that make them dangerous?

SLOW LORIS FACT BOX

SPECIES NAME: *Nycticebus coucang*
LENGTH: Up to 15 inches long
FOUND: Tropical rainforests of Southeast Asia

This slow loris looks cute, fluffy, and very cuddly—but looks can be deceptive. It doesn't have spines or stings, but it does make a foul stink to warn attackers that it has another secret weapon!

Sit and watch

Vampire bat

A vampire bat uses razor sharp teeth to cut into a victim's flesh and grooves on its tongue help it channel the blood that it laps up. Poison in their saliva enters the victim's blood supply and stops it from clotting, so the wound keeps bleeding. Vampire bats don't want to kill their victims, so the poison isn't lethal.

Vampire bats don't prey on humans. They feed on the blood of cows and horses.

Back away slowly

Duck-billed platypus

Male platypuses fight each other at mating time. They have venomous claws, called spurs, on their hind legs that they use to slash at each other. The venom causes extreme pain in humans who get in their way, but it's not deadly.

Platypuses have super-soft fur, but these mammals don't like cuddling so they are best left alone!

Although a slow loris's bite can be deadly, some people like to keep these endangered animals as pets.

RUN FOR YOUR LIFE!

Slow loris

A slow loris has special glands on its arms that make smelly, toxic oil. As it cleans its fur, the oil gets spread around its body and onto its teeth. If the loris is scared, or wants to fight a rival, it can go from slow to speedy in seconds, sinking its teeth into a victim with painful—and sometimes terrible—results.

GLOSSARY

AMPHIBIAN
A type of animal that lays eggs and spends part of its life in water and part of its life on land. Frogs, toads, and newts are all amphibians.

ANTIVENIN
A medicine that is used to stop venom from working

ARACHNOLOGIST
A person who studies spiders. The study of spiders is called arachnology.

BARB
A spike or spine that has a hook on it, so it's difficult to remove

CAMOUFLAGE
Colors and patterns that help an animal to hide

DORSAL FIN
The fin on the back, or upperside, of a fish

FANG
A sharp, pointed tooth

FIN
Part of a fish's body that is used to swim, change direction, and keep its balance

INSECT
A small animal that has three pairs of legs and a tough skin

INVERTEBRATE
An animal that does not have bones or a skeleton

LETHAL
Something that is lethal can cause a human or animal to die

MAMMAL
A type of animal that has fur or hair and feeds its young with milk

MARINE
Something that is marine is found in the sea

MOLLUSK
A type of invertebrate. Some mollusks have shells, but others have soft bodies. Many mollusks live in the sea.

PREDATOR
An animal that hunts other animals to eat

PREY
An animal that is hunted and eaten by predators

REPTILE
A type of animal that has a tough, scaly skin. Many reptiles lay eggs. Lizards, snakes, turtles, and crocodiles are all reptiles.

SALIVA
This is another word for spit

TENTACLE
A slender, bendy body part that an animal uses to touch and feel, and sometimes to taste and smell too

TOXIC
Something that is toxic is poisonous

VENOM
A poison made in the body of some animals. It is injected into another animal, usually by teeth, spines, stings, or claws.

INDEX

Picture credits:
(t=top, b=bottom, l=left, r=right, c=center, fc=front cover, bc=back cover)

Alamy
8t imageBROKER, 10-11b WorldFoto, 11c imageBROKER, 14-15t VPC Animals Photo, 14-15c Arco Images GMBH, 15b National Geographic Image Collection, 18-19b Yuval Halfman, 19t Matthijs Kuijpers, 19c All Canada Photos, 20t NK Sanford, 20b Rolf Nussbaumer Photography, 22-23t Blickwinkel, 23c Ken Griffiths, 24t Gerard Lacz, 25 Blickwinkel, 29 Minden Pictures, 30-31 Zuma Press Inc.

FLPA
3b John Holmes, 5t Daniel Heuclin/Biosphoto, 16b Hiroya Minakuchi/Minden Pictures, 23b Photo Researchers,

Getty
6-7t Eric Feferberg, 16t ullstein bild,

Nature Picture Library
26-27t Barry Mansell

Shutterstock
fc 1 aulia ananta, 2t belizar, 2b pym.2p, 4b Dennis W Donohue, 5b Kostiantyn Kravchenko, 6-7c EmBaSy, 7b Dr Morley Read, 8b Dennis W Donohue, 9 Dr Morley Read, 11t MR BUDDEE WIANGNGORN, 11t Cora Unk Photo, 12t Bildagentur Zoonar GmbH, 12b YUSRAN ABDUL RAHMAN, 13 Gino Santa Maria, 17 Coralie Mathieu, 21 Aleksey Stemmer, 24b Ken Griffiths, 26-27b Sainam51, 26-27b W. Phokin, 27c Susan Flashman, 28t SaveJungle, 28b TOSP, bc BaracaPix